CORNERSTONES OF FREEDOM™

The OREGON TRAIL

BY MEL FRIEDMAN

CHILDREN'S PRESS®

An Imprint of Scholastic Inc.

New York   Toronto   London   Auckland   Sydney
Mexico City   New Delhi   Hong Kong
Danbury, Connecticut

Content Consultant
James Marten, PhD
Professor and Chair,
History Department
Marquette University
Milwaukee, Wisconsin

Library of Congress Cataloging-in-Publication Data

Friedman, Mel, 1946–
 The Oregon Trail/by Mel Friedman.
   p. cm.—(Cornerstones of freedom)
 Includes bibliographical references and index.
 ISBN-13: 978-0-531-23063-3 (lib. bdg.)
 ISBN-13: 978-0-531-28163-5 (pbk.)
 1. Oregon National Historic Trail—Juvenile literature. 2. Frontier
and pioneer life—West (U.S.)—Juvenile literature. 3. Overland
journeys to the Pacific—Juvenile literature. 4. Pioneers—Oregon
National Historic Trail—History—19th century—Juvenile literature.
5. West (U.S.)—History—19th century—Juvenile literature. 6. Oregon
Territory—History—Juvenile literature. I. Title.
 F597.F75 2012
 917.804'2—dc23   2012000496

Photographs © 2013: Alamy Images: 41 (Greg Ryan), 54 (Greg Vaughn), 20
(Niday Picture Library); AP Images/North Wind Picture Archives: 6, 21, 33,
36, 40, 42, 48, 55; Bridgeman Art Library: 39 (Newell Convers Wyeth/Private
Collection/Christie's Images), 32 (Newell Convers Wyeth/Private Collection/
Peter Newark American Pictures), 25 (Severino Baraldi/Private Collection/
Look and Learn), 16 (Thomas Mickell Burnham/Private Collection); Corbis
Images/E. Boyd Smith/Blue Lantern Studio: 18; Getty Images: 14 (Apic), 4
bottom, 29 (Peter Stackpole/Time & Life Pictures); Library of Congress: 47
(Charles Fenderich), 45, 57 (John Sartain/Thomas Sully), 8 (L. Prang & Co.,
Boston); National Geographic Stock/Phil Schermeister: back cover, cover;
Shutterstock, Inc.: 4 top, 27 (Christopher Poliquin), 5 bottom, 37 (Jean-
Edouard Rozey), 7 (Mariusz S. Jurdielewicz), 34 (Patricia Hofmeester); State
of Oregon Legislative Administration: 15; Superstock, Inc./Vittorio Bianchini:
13, 56; The Granger Collection: 22 (C.W. Jefferys), 10 (Charles Willson Peale),
11, 35 (Currier & Ives), 30, 58 (N.C. Wyeth), 2, 3, 23 (William Tylee Ranney), 5
top, 17, 24, 26, 28, 38, 44, 46, 49, 50, 51, 59.

Maps by XNR Productions, Inc.

BRINGING HISTORY to LIFE

Did you know that studying history can be fun?

BRING HISTORY TO LIFE by becoming a history investigator. Examine the evidence (primary and secondary source materials); cross-examine the people and witnesses. Take a look at what was happening at the time—but be careful! What happened years ago might suddenly become incredibly interesting and change the way you think!

Contents

From Sea to Shining Sea

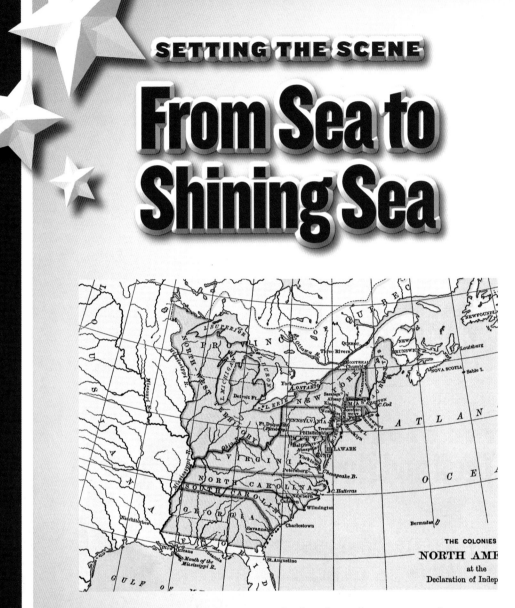

THE COLONIES
NORTH AME
at the
Declaration of Indep

In 1803, the United States stretched only as far west as the Mississippi River.

The song "America the Beautiful" is often called the unofficial national anthem of the United States. It celebrates the American spirit and the beauty of a land that stretches "from sea to shining sea." But the nation did not always stretch all the way from the East Coast to the West Coast. It wasn't until 1846 that Americans were able to travel from coast to coast without leaving U.S. soil. By 1853, the country's mainland, which excludes Alaska and Hawaii, was shaped as it is today.

In 1803, however, the nation had only 17 states. It was one-third of its present size. Its western boundary was the Mississippi River, and most of its citizens lived along the Atlantic coast. West of the Mississippi were lands inhabited by native peoples, but claimed by European countries. At the time, it was uncertain if U.S. borders would one day touch two oceans. The key to such expansion would be the Oregon Trail.

Today, the United States reaches from the Atlantic Ocean to the Pacific Ocean.

THE FIRST JOURNEY WEST

Christopher Columbus was the first of many European explorers to visit North America.

Explorer Christopher

Columbus's arrival in the Americas in 1492 set off a scramble among European countries to build **colonies** there. One of the main purposes of these colonies was to find gold, silver, furs, and other riches to ship back to their home countries. By the mid-17th century, Spain, France, the Netherlands, and Great Britain had settlements dotting the Atlantic coast. France also claimed a huge territory along the Mississippi River. Still farther west, the Spanish flag flew over what are now California and the American Southwest. In 1784, fur traders founded a Russian colony in present-day Alaska.

The American Revolution ended in victory for the newly formed United States.

A New Frontier

In the 18th century, wars in Europe and the Americas rearranged the colonial map of North America. The most important war to occur in the colonies was the American Revolution (1775-1783). It resulted in 13 British colonies declaring independence and forming the United States of America. The agreement ending the war awarded the United States all British land east of the Mississippi River.

The war greatly reduced Great Britain's power in North

America. But Britain still held Canada and was determined to push that colony's borders westward. The British were also eager to grab areas of the huge territory in the Pacific Northwest known as Oregon Country.

Following the war, Americans began moving west into the rich farmlands won from the British. Settlements sprang up quickly. The Mississippi River became America's newest **frontier**. But the Americans would soon have more land to explore.

In 1803, France offered to sell the United States all the land it owned west of the Mississippi River. This area was called the Louisiana Territory. It covered 828,000 square miles (2,144,510 square kilometers) extending west to

The Mississippi River became an important shipping route as the United States expanded westward.

A VIEW FROM ABROAD

Between 1762 and 1800, ownership of the Louisiana Territory was traded back and forth between Spain and France. It was under French control when Thomas Jefferson became president in 1801. French leader Napoléon Bonaparte hoped to make Louisiana part of an expanded French empire in the Western Hemisphere. But a slave revolt in Haiti crippled his army and cost France a great deal of money. Napoléon decided to focus on conquering Europe instead of expanding in North America. He determined that the best way to fund his efforts in Europe was to sell the Louisiana Territory.

the Rocky Mountains. President Thomas Jefferson leaped at the opportunity to expand the United States westward. The deal instantly doubled the country's size.

Man with a Vision

Jefferson had long been curious about the immense wilderness west of the Mississippi. No white men had explored it thoroughly. Some of its geography, resources, plants, and wildlife were unknown. Only rumors and legends offered clues about what wonders it might contain.

Jefferson believed that it was America's destiny to expand westward to the Pacific Ocean. He had tried three times previously, without success, to launch an **expedition** westward. Now that he was president and the United States owned Louisiana, he was finally able to

THOMAS JEFFERSON'S INSTRUCTIONS TO LEWIS AND CLARK

In a letter to Meriwether Lewis dated June 20, 1803, President Thomas Jefferson drew up instructions for the Lewis and Clark expedition. See page 60 for a link to view Jefferson's letter online.

send a team of explorers across the land. That team was the famed Corps of Discovery, headed by Meriwether Lewis and William Clark.

Thomas Jefferson had long dreamed of exploring the western portion of North America.

George Vancouver was one of the first European explorers to visit the Pacific Northwest.

Buried Coins

One of the many reasons for the expedition was that Great Britain was rapidly expanding into the Pacific Northwest. In the early 1790s, British explorer George Vancouver had visited and mapped sites on the Oregon coast. In 1793, Britain's Alexander Mackenzie traveled through Canada becoming the first white person to cross the continent. These events established Great Britain's claims to western Canada and parts of Oregon.

Before 1803, only one American visit in Oregon stood out. In 1792, Captain Robert Gray became the first person to sail into Oregon along the Columbia River. He went ashore and buried some coins to prove he had been there.

Gray's achievement gave the United States its first claim to Oregon. Jefferson was counting on Lewis and Clark to build on Gray's claim and prevent Great Britain from taking control of Oregon.

SPOTLIGHT ON

Robert Gray

Born in Rhode Island, Robert Gray had a career of many firsts. In 1790, he became the first American to sail all the way around the world. He was among the first Americans to participate in the fur trade with China. Gray is also credited with an important scientific achievement. Measurements he made in Oregon in 1792 established for the first time that the North American continent was about 3,000 miles (4,828 km) wide. Gray's voyage into Oregon was later a basis for U.S. claims to the area.

Under Way

On May 21, 1804, the Corps of Discovery left St. Louis, Missouri, to begin its journey westward. Nearly four dozen men climbed into three boats packed with supplies and headed north up the Missouri River through the Great Plains. Progress was slow. In October, the corps reached what is now North Dakota. Knowing that the river would soon freeze, the men camped for the winter near a Native American village.

In the spring, the journey resumed. By autumn, the corps had cleared the steep Rocky Mountains and descended into Oregon Country, where the men followed the mighty Columbia River west. By mid-November 1805, the Corps of Discovery had reached the Pacific Ocean.

The corps had succeeded in blazing a trail that stretched from St. Louis across the American wilderness to the Pacific coast. The men had also carried the U.S. flag over the Rockies into parts of Oregon Country that no European explorer had ever seen or claimed.

On their journey westward, Lewis and Clark encountered plant and animal species they had never seen before.

Paradise on the Pacific

After wintering on the Oregon coast, the Corps of Discovery retraced its path back to St. Louis, arriving on September 23, 1806. Its members were welcomed as heroes. To Jefferson's delight, Lewis and Clark had returned with detailed journals of their journey. These journals contained hundreds of pages of notes and drawings, supplying information about western lands, native peoples, plants, and animals. They also included detailed maps drawn by William Clark. Thousands of **pioneers** on the Oregon Trail would soon use these maps to guide them on the journey west.

William Clark made detailed drawings of many animal and plant species.

CHAPTER 2

BLAZING THE TRAIL

Lewis and Clark made it across the Rocky Mountains, but the journey was difficult.

BEFORE THE LEWIS AND CLARK

expedition, many Americans had believed that the geography of the West was relatively simple. The Corps of Discovery proved this assumption wrong. The surface features of the West varied wildly and presented many dangers. There were several steep mountain ranges to cross and punishing distances to walk on the way to the Pacific Ocean. The only pass the corps had found through the Rocky Mountains was too narrow for wagons. People could travel the Lewis and Clark trail on horseback. But this difficult path was not suitable for families traveling with children, possessions, and **livestock**.

Neither Britain nor the United States was a clear winner in the War of 1812, which ended in a stalemate.

A New Trail

A search soon began for another path that would allow wagons across the Rockies. The Oregon Trail was not blazed all at once. Instead, it was stitched together piece by piece over many decades. It wasn't until the 1840s that large numbers of pioneers began traveling on this dusty trail to opportunity.

Between 1812 and 1815, the United States fought another war with Great Britain. After the war, the two countries agreed to share ownership of Oregon. Many Americans saw this as a good reason to travel there.

Fur traders were some of the first Americans to travel to Oregon along the Lewis and Clark trail. In 1812, a fur trader named Robert Stuart was in the middle of a journey back East from Oregon when he stumbled upon a gap in the Rockies wide enough for wagons to travel through. His find came to be known as South Pass because it was south of the smaller gap that Lewis and Clark had found.

The South Pass made it possible for wagons to cross the Rocky Mountains.

The Fur Trade

Beaver skins sold for a very high price in the 1800s. They were used to make expensive waterproof hats and capes. Beavers were so valuable that trappers called them "brown gold." Furs made John Jacob Astor the richest man in America after he set up a trading company along the Columbia River in 1811. As traders began to run out of beavers in the East, they moved farther and farther west in search of the small, brown rodents. Many of these traders began heading to Oregon after learning that the Pacific Northwest was swarming with beavers. Over time, the fur traders' well-worn path westward became the Oregon Trail.

Stuart was the first person to travel the entire length of the Oregon Trail, but he did it by going in the opposite direction that later pioneers would travel. Oddly, Stuart did not make his discovery public. South Pass remained unknown to most Americans for another 12 years.

Mountain Men

The fur trade also gave rise to a new breed of American known as the mountain man. Mountain men were fur traders and explorers. They were independent, rugged, and fearless, but uncomfortable in regular society. They were also skilled with weapons and knew how to survive alone in the wilderness. Over the next 30 years, mountain men traveled back and forth across the Oregon Trail. They found new paths that would make travel easier for later pioneers.

Mountain men were among the first pioneers to travel along the Oregon Trail.

Jedediah Smith was one of the best-known mountain men. As a teenager, he had been inspired by the journals of Lewis and Clark. In 1822, at the age of 23, Smith

A FIRSTHAND LOOK AT
THE AD THAT TAMED THE ROCKIES

On February 13, 1822, a short advertisement appeared in the *Missouri Gazette & Public Advertiser*. Businessman William H. Ashley was hiring 100 men to venture into the Rockies to trap beavers and otters. Jedediah Smith and Jim Bridger were among the men who answered the ad. See page 60 for a link to view the ad online.

joined a fur-trapping company in the Rockies. Two years later, he rediscovered Robert Stuart's South Pass and led his men across. By 1828, Smith had made the first recorded crossing of the Sierra Nevada mountain range and the first land journey up the California coast to Oregon.

Further Exploration

Between the early 1800s and the mid-1840s, mountain men and U.S. military missions had explored almost every corner of the West. The once nearly blank map of North America's interior was filling in, sometimes with unexpected results.

Explorer Zebulon Pike and his men traveled into New Mexico, where they were captured by Spanish officials and sent back into U.S. territory.

John Colter was a member of the Corps of Discovery before becoming a mountain man.

In 1806, a government mission under Lieutenant Zebulon Pike scouted the Great Plains and the Rockies. Pike reported that much of the West was like the "sandy deserts of Africa."

In 1808, mountain man John Colter made his way into an area where mud boiled and steaming water shot straight up into the air. No one believed him when he reported what he had seen. People joked that he'd found "Colter's Hell." But Colter had actually been the first white person to observe the **geysers** and hot springs of what is now Yellowstone National Park in Wyoming.

Stephen H. Long met with Pawnee Indians during his expedition into the Rocky Mountains.

From 1819 to 1820, Major Stephen H. Long led an expedition of scientists into the Rockies. He backed Pike's belief that the lands between the upper Mississippi and the Rockies were a "great American desert" that would be impossible to farm. Some historians believe that this mistaken judgment delayed settlement of the Great Plains for 30 years.

In 1824, mountain man Jim Bridger sailed down the Bear River in Utah until he reached a huge body of water. He believed that he had reached the Pacific Ocean. He had actually come upon the Great Salt Lake.

By the late 1830s, fur traders had nearly wiped out the most prized fur-bearing animals in the West. Silk had replaced beaver fur as the popular clothing material back East, and many fur-trading companies began to close down. One era was ending, but a new one was beginning. Small groups of ordinary Americans had begun testing and traveling the Oregon Trail.

Milestones

Missionaries were among the first Americans to begin traveling west after the mountain men and the military cleared a path. Missionaries had long been interested in spreading Christianity among Native Americans in Oregon. But few dared to make the journey there at first. Only seasoned explorers and mountain men had

TODAY'S PERSPECTIVE

During his expedition in the West, Zebulon Pike saw a tall mountain in Colorado. The mountain was later named after Pike. The legal name of this famous mountain is Pikes Peak instead of Pike's Peak. Since 1890, the U.S. government has discouraged the use of possessive apostrophes in the names of locations. Only five so far have been allowed. In 1978, Colorado passed a law ordering that Pikes Peak always be spelled without an apostrophe.

mastered the trail. No one was sure if heavily loaded pioneer wagons could make it all the way to Oregon. Some doubted that women and children could survive the ordeal.

In 1830, Jedediah Smith and his partner William Sublette piloted the first wagon train on a 500-mile (805 km) trip across the Rockies at South Pass. Two years later, a U.S. military officer led 110 soldiers and ox-drawn wagons on a test run of the trail that ended in southeastern Washington, just short of its goal. A few missionaries were encouraged by these breakthroughs. They decided to chance the trip. By 1834, a tiny community of missionaries had formed in northwestern Oregon. All of the missionaries living there were men.

Oregon settlements grew larger as more Americans moved west.

Narcissa Whitman (left) and Eliza Spalding established mission schools while living among Native Americans.

In 1836, two female missionaries, Narcissa Whitman and Eliza Spalding, proved that women could handle the trail as well as men could. They became the first white women to cross the Rockies and reach Oregon.

The first true pioneer wagon train left Missouri in 1841. Former mountain man Thomas Fitzpatrick led the group westward. The wagon train split up near Fort Hall in what is now Idaho. One party turned southwest to go to California. The other continued northwest to Oregon.

Average Americans were now able to travel the Oregon Trail. It wasn't long before "Oregon fever" began spreading across America like wildfire.

CHAPTER 3

OREGON OR BUST!

Tales of settlement in the West captured the imaginations of Americans in the East.

EXCITEMENT ABOUT OREGON

Country had been building steadily ever since the Corps of Discovery's return to St. Louis. The excitement grew to a frenzy during the late 1830s and early 1840s. Word spread about the wonders and attractions of this region. Hungry for land, many ordinary Americans saw the West as a place of opportunity. They heard that the weather was mild and sicknesses were rare in Oregon. They also heard that the air and water were clean and that land was free for the taking.

Many people also believed that westward expansion was a patriotic act. They reasoned that if enough Americans settled in Oregon, the British would be forced to leave.

YESTERDAY'S HEADLINES

"Oregon fever" was a major story in many newspapers in the early 1840s. The March 8, 1843, issue of the *Cleveland Plain Dealer* described Oregon as "a land of pure delight in the woody solitudes of the West." On April 26, 1843, the *Ohio Statesman* reported: "Oregon fever is raging in almost every part of the Union....It is reasonable to suppose that there will be at least five thousand Americans west of the Rocky Mountains by next autumn." Articles such as these helped spread the word of Oregon's potential and encouraged even more Americans to think about moving west along the Oregon Trail.

The Great Migration

At daybreak on May 22, 1843, a shot rang out over a campground near Independence, Missouri. It was the wake-up signal for 1,000 men, women, and children. Sleepy pioneers tumbled out of their tents and wagons and began preparing for the day's journey. Around 120 wagons soon fell into a line three-quarters of a mile (1.2 km) long.

The signal was given to roll out. Large iron-tired wagons creaked as the wagon train slowly made its way onto the prairie. The Great **Migration** of pioneers to the new frontier had begun. For more than two decades, wagon trains just like this one would rumble west over the same tire tracks each spring.

The Oregon Trail started at any of several points on the Missouri River and ended 2,124 miles (3,418 km) away in Oregon City. Pioneers could also take branches of the trail to present-day Washington, Idaho, Utah, or California. The amount of traffic along the Oregon Trail spiked when gold was discovered in California in 1848.

Depending on one's destination, the trip usually took between four and six months. Pioneers began their trips in spring so that they would arrive before the harsh winter began. Any wagons that had not crossed the mountain passes before winter were almost certainly doomed.

Thousands of people traveled to California during the gold rush, which began in 1848.

Prairie schooners were usually just large enough to hold a pioneer family's possessions.

Pioneers traveled in small farm wagons that they covered with durable cloth. These wagons were often called prairie schooners because their bowed canvas tops made them look like windblown sailboats.

A FIRSTHAND LOOK AT
THE FRÉMONT REPORT

Many pioneers were inspired to move west after reading reports and journals by earlier explorers. One of the most popular reports was John Frémont's account of his trip along the Oregon Trail in 1842 and 1843. The book was a best seller for 15 years. See page 60 for a link to read the Frémont Report online.

Heavy Loads

Six to eight oxen pulled each wagon. An average wagon, when fully loaded, could weigh up to 2,500 pounds (1,134 kilograms). Every inch of wagon space was carefully organized to make room for food, water, tools, supplies, and belongings. That left no room inside for passengers. Everyone except for those who were sick, injured, elderly, or pregnant walked the entire distance to Oregon. One pioneer wore out nine pairs of new shoes on her march.

Circumstances often forced pioneers to lighten their loads by dumping possessions by the side of the trail. These items came to be called "leeverites," as in "leave 'er right there!"

Pioneers often traveled together in large groups.

The Oregon Trail hugged close to the banks of major river systems for as long as possible. Access to fresh water was a matter of life and death for the pioneers. But crossing these rivers presented serious challenges. Rivers often had to be **forded**. Other times, pioneers hired Native American ferrymen to paddle them across the water. Pioneers also built makeshift rafts or waterproofed their wagons and removed the wheels so that they could paddle them across.

Pioneers jokingly described the Platte River, which cuts across the Great Plains, as "a mile wide and six inches deep." Even so, wading across it was no laughing matter. Its muddy bottom hid pools of quicksand that could swallow up a man or even an ox. To make things worse, many pioneers couldn't swim. In 1850 alone, 37 people drowned while trying to cross the dangerous Green River in Wyoming.

Crossing rivers was one of the most difficult parts of the journey west.

Pioneers saw many memorable sights on the trail. They passed through expanses of wildflowers and saw prairie dogs popping in and out of holes in the ground. They also marveled at the vast herds of bison that roamed the plains.

Rock Stars

Leaving the grassy plains, pioneers entered a landscape dotted by strange and wonderful rock formations. The most famous of these **landmarks** was Chimney Rock, located in what became Nebraska. This huge, reddish rock was topped by a stone "chimney" more than 120 feet (37 meters) high. It could be seen from 40 miles (64 km) away. Chimney Rock marked the end of the march across flatlands and the beginning of the slow, steady climb up the Rockies.

SPOTLIGHT ON

Bison

The American bison, a type of wild ox, once reigned as "king of the plains." Bison are good swimmers. They are also surprisingly nimble and fast. Bison can reach top running speeds of about 40 miles (64 km) per hour. Although normally peaceful, bison have been known to attack without warning, using their massive heads as battering rams.

An estimated 50 million bison roamed North America before the 1800s. By the late 1800s, American hunters had reduced the population to near extinction. Today, after years of protection, herds have recovered. The American bison is no longer endangered, but its numbers are still much smaller than they once were.

Circled wagons provided a protective barrier for the pioneers to hide behind in case they were attacked by outsiders, and prevented horses, livestock, and other animals from running off while the pioneers slept.

March! March! March!

Daily life on the Oregon Trail was hard. Everything centered on keeping the wagon train moving. The wagon train leader, or pilot, set the pace of the march. Wagons were unloaded every evening to prepare for eating and sleeping. They had to be reloaded every morning before the march could resume. In between, wagons were repaired, animals were fed and watered, and cows were milked.

Pioneers awoke at sunrise and pitched camp before sundown. On good days, they walked as many as 15 miles (24 km). Camping areas were usually formed by arranging the wagons in a circle. This was done for protection and to fence in animals for the night. Some wagon trains rested on Sundays.

Meals were not fancy on the Oregon Trail. The standard menu for breakfast, lunch, and dinner was coffee, bacon, beans, and stale bread or flapjacks. Pioneers occasionally spiced up these meals with bison or antelope meat from hunts or with dried fish or vegetables purchased from Native Americans.

Hard Times

Building campfires was difficult on the journey west. Few trees grew along the Oregon Trail. The ones that did were felled for firewood by the first waves of pioneers. Later pioneers had to burn dried bison droppings called buffalo

There was little time to rest on the Oregon Trail.

Women with babies were among the few people who rode inside wagons.

chips in place of wood. Children were responsible for gathering these chips in baskets during the day.

Women had especially hard lives on the trail. Many had had no say in the decision to move west. The trip required them to look after the children and the ill, do chores, and still find the energy to keep pace with the men on the march. Sometimes women also had to herd cattle or drive the teams of mules or oxen that pulled the wagons.

Teenage girls helped with traditional female chores, such as cooking and caring for children. Some also learned to ride horses and drive wagons. Teenage boys were usually responsible for feeding the livestock and driving the wagons. Sometimes they also hunted with the men.

Many pioneers began their journey in fear of attacks from Native Americans. But such attacks rarely happened. Most native groups actually helped the pioneers. Less than 1 percent of the estimated 20,000 to 30,000 deaths on the trail between 1835 and 1855 resulted from attacks by Native Americans.

The greatest threats to health and safety were floods, stampedes, and deadly diseases such as **cholera**, smallpox, and influenza. These diseases could pass quickly from one member of a wagon train to another. Cholera was the single biggest killer on the trail. It can kill a healthy person in just 24 hours. Historians believe that about 10 percent of the pioneers died before reaching their intended destinations.

Pioneers often left behind grave markers for family members who died along the trail.

CHAPTER 4

THE END OF THE TRAIL

Americans established several towns in the Pacific Northwest in the 1840s, even before the United States owned the territory.

THE OREGON TRAIL AND ITS

branches brought waves of settlers to the Pacific Northwest, California, and Utah. When the Great Migration began in 1843, none of these areas belonged to the United States. Mexico controlled California and the Southwest. Great Britain shared Oregon Country in an uneasy partnership with the United States.

Many settlers began traveling to southwestern towns such as Santa Fe, New Mexico, in the mid-1800s.

All of that changed in just a few years. Great Britain and the United States agreed to divide up Oregon Country's 500,000 square miles (1,300,000 sq km). Texas, California, and most of today's American Southwest also became part of the United States. These new lands were not gained without a struggle, though.

"Fifty-Four Forty or Fight!"

Political pressure had been building for years to solve what was called the "Oregon question." The United States claimed all of Oregon up to a line on the map fixed at 54°40' north **latitude**, well beyond today's

Canadian border. Great Britain claimed all of Oregon down to California's northern border. Talks aimed at drawing a line somewhere in between had repeatedly broken down.

James K. Polk won the U.S. presidential race in 1844. He ran on a campaign slogan of "Fifty-four forty or fight!" And after taking office, Polk began making warlike statements, calling the British "intruders" in Oregon. This all suggested that he would rather go to war with Great Britain than compromise on Oregon.

U.S. control of Oregon was an important issue in James K. Polk's presidential campaign.

The Mexican Connection

President Polk proved to be someone who was not afraid to take other's territory by force. A decade earlier, American settlers in Texas had revolted against Mexico and set up their own government. They hoped to one day join the United States. Their wish came true in 1845, during Polk's presidency, when the United States **annexed** Texas.

This act led to a war between Mexico and the United States that lasted from 1846 until 1848. President Polk and supporters of **Manifest Destiny** welcomed the war. Victory brought California and most of the Southwest under U.S. control.

U.S. general Zachary Taylor led an invasion of Mexico during the Mexican-American War.

Avoiding War

The British watched these developments closely. They were not eager to wage a war in the West. Their spies had reported that the American population in Oregon was growing quickly. They also predicted that the Americans there would put up a fierce fight for their land.

In America, political support for war was strong in the Midwest, the region from which most pioneers came. But most people in the Northeast and South were against going to war with Great Britain. Polk slowly realized that it would be foolish to clash with Great Britain while a war with Mexico was still in progress.

YESTERDAY'S HEADLINES

On December 2, 1845, an editorial in the *New York Tribune* rejected President Polk's charge that Great Britain was an "intruder" with no valid claims to Oregon. It stated that "Great Britain claims Oregon on just such grounds as our claim rests upon—Discovery, Exploration, Settlement, Possession.... Great Britain's right to her portion of the Continent is as strong and as just as ours to what belongs to us."

The *New York Herald* agreed with Polk's statements. On January 26, 1846, the paper's editor urged the government to think bigger and take even bolder actions to expand the country. He wrote that the United States should "annex the whole of Mexico, instead of California— to merge the two republics in one, instead of taking a slice for breakfast today and another for dinner tomorrow."

A VIEW FROM ABROAD

The British press was highly critical of the United States, especially how it treated native populations as westward expansion continued. An editorial in the *Times of London* on January 19, 1846, stated that "[W]e know that whenever [the United States'] pioneers advance, the existing rights of other nations and other races are annihilated. They found their future power upon the extirpation [elimination] of their rivals, and the perpetual bondage of their slaves."

A deal with Great Britain was finally struck in June 1846. Oregon Country was split up at the 49th parallel. Great Britain took the northern part. It later became the Canadian province of British Columbia. The United States got the southern part, which was renamed the Oregon Territory in 1848.

The United States took control of the Northwest and Southwest territories in the mid-1800s.

Salt Lake City, Utah, was founded in 1847 by Mormon settlers looking for religious freedom in the West.

In 1859, Oregon was admitted to the Union as the thirty-third state. The remaining parts of the territory became the states of Washington (in 1889) and Idaho (in 1890).

Golden Spike

From the start of the Great Migration to the beginning of the Civil War in 1861, nearly 500,000 pioneers walked the Oregon Trail. About two-thirds of them were lured to California by the gleam of gold. The rest settled in Oregon and Utah in roughly equal numbers.

The telegraph allowed people to easily communicate with one another across the country.

By mid-century, the United States was very different from what it had been before the Louisiana Purchase. New technologies linked the vast nation town to town and from sea to sea. Steamboats chugged along the country's rivers. Canals, bridges, and roads made travel faster and easier. People sent almost instant messages over **telegraph** wires.

On May 10, 1869, a golden spike was driven into the ground near the Great Salt Lake in Utah. The spike marked the completion of the first **transcontinental**

In 1966, the U.S. government declared the Oregon Trail to be a National Historic Trail. Visitors can walk along 2,000 miles (3,200 km) of the original trail to see exactly where pioneers once traveled on their journey west. See page 60 for a link to more information about visiting the trail.

railway line. With the opening of railway traffic to the West, there was no longer a need for dangerous, dust-choked wagon travel.

The completion of the transcontinental railroad was celebrated with a ceremony at Promontory Summit, Utah.

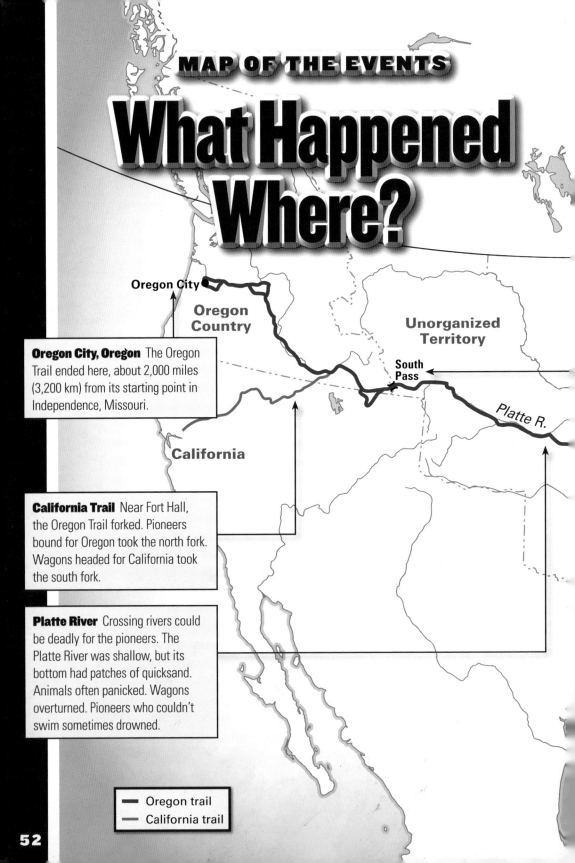

What Happened Where?

Oregon City

Oregon Country

Unorganized Territory

South Pass

Oregon City, Oregon The Oregon Trail ended here, about 2,000 miles (3,200 km) from its starting point in Independence, Missouri.

Platte R.

California

California Trail Near Fort Hall, the Oregon Trail forked. Pioneers bound for Oregon took the north fork. Wagons headed for California took the south fork.

Platte River Crossing rivers could be deadly for the pioneers. The Platte River was shallow, but its bottom had patches of quicksand. Animals often panicked. Wagons overturned. Pioneers who couldn't swim sometimes drowned.

— Oregon trail
— California trail

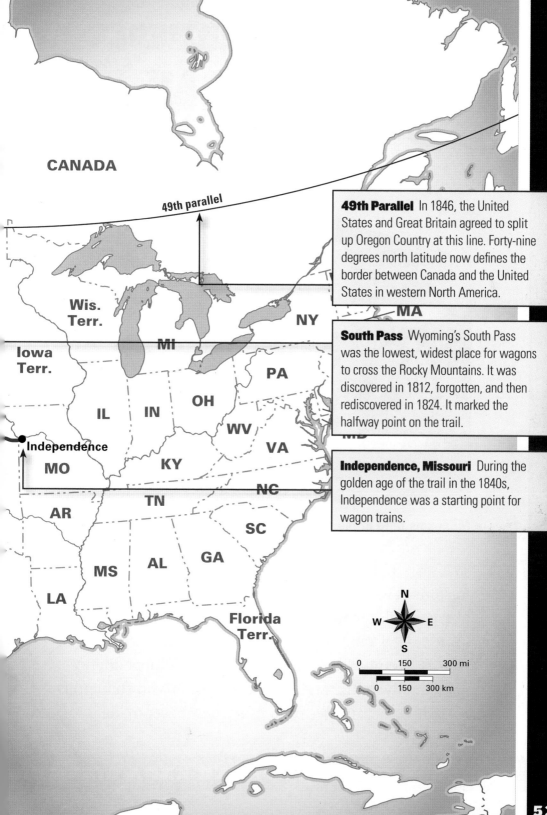

CANADA

49th parallel

49th Parallel In 1846, the United States and Great Britain agreed to split up Oregon Country at this line. Forty-nine degrees north latitude now defines the border between Canada and the United States in western North America.

Wis. Terr.

Iowa Terr.

NY

MI

MA

PA

OH

IL

IN

WV

South Pass Wyoming's South Pass was the lowest, widest place for wagons to cross the Rocky Mountains. It was discovered in 1812, forgotten, and then rediscovered in 1824. It marked the halfway point on the trail.

Independence

VA

MO

KY

Independence, Missouri During the golden age of the trail in the 1840s, Independence was a starting point for wagon trains.

NC

AR

TN

SC

MS

AL

GA

LA

Florida Terr.

N
W   E
S

0   150   300 mi
0   150   300 km

Museums help preserve the history of the Oregon Trail.

The story of the Oregon Trail lives on in memory and in stone. Visitors to many of the historic sites along the trail can still see the grooves worn into the ground by hundreds of thousands of iron-tired pioneer wagons. Names of emigrants can still be read on Independence Rock in Wyoming. Many of the pioneers who so happily scratched their names onto its surface never made it to

IN 1906, FORMER PIONEER EZRA MEEKER

their destinations. The crude markers used to honor their graves are still visible in places on the trail.

But the pioneers' march westward also took a toll on the land. It wiped out almost all fur-bearing animals such as the bison, which were key to Native American survival. Few Americans in the 1800s gave much thought to the destruction they were causing. Before 1800, many Native Americans lived on the North American plains. But pioneers forced them to move again and again as the United States expanded. While there were positive results to the country's expansion, there were also many negative consequences that the country continues to deal with today.

Settlers in the West hunted bison for food, as well as for sport.

INFLUENTIAL INDIVIDUALS

Thomas Jefferson

Thomas Jefferson (1743–1826) was the third president of the United States. In 1803, he ordered the purchase of the Louisiana Territory from France, which doubled the size of the United States.

Robert Gray (1755–1806) was an American trader and explorer who sailed around the world twice and was the first person to sail into the Columbia River. This gave America its first claim to Oregon.

John Jacob Astor (1763–1848) was a German-born American who became fabulously wealthy from the fur trade on the Pacific coast.

William Clark (1770–1838) co-captained the Corps of Discovery with Meriwether Lewis. He made excellent maps that pioneers used years later on the Oregon Trail.

Meriwether Lewis (1774–1809) was an American soldier and explorer who led the Lewis and Clark expedition along with William Clark. He served as governor of the Louisiana Territory from 1806 to 1809.

Robert Stuart (1785–1848) was the first person to blaze the Oregon Trail. He traveled the trail from west to east in 1812. In the process, he discovered South Pass through the Rockies. Unfortunately, his discovery was forgotten until 1824.

James K. Polk

James K. Polk (1795–1849) was the eleventh president of the United States. He was a strong believer in Manifest Destiny. In 1846, he signed an agreement with Great Britain that ended a long Oregon border dispute and established the 49th parallel as America's northern border with Canada in the West.

Jedediah Smith (1798–1831) was an American trailblazer and fur trader. In 1824, he rediscovered Robert Stuart's South Pass. It became the gateway to the West for tens of thousands of pioneers.

TIMELINE

1792

Robert Gray becomes the first explorer to enter the Columbia River.

1803

The United States purchases the Louisiana Territory from France.

1824

Jedediah Smith rediscovers Stuart's long-forgotten South Pass.

1830

The first wagon train crosses the Rocky Mountains.

1846

The United States and Great Britain decide to divide Oregon at the 49th parallel.

1848

The California gold rush begins, increasing traffic on the Oregon Trail.

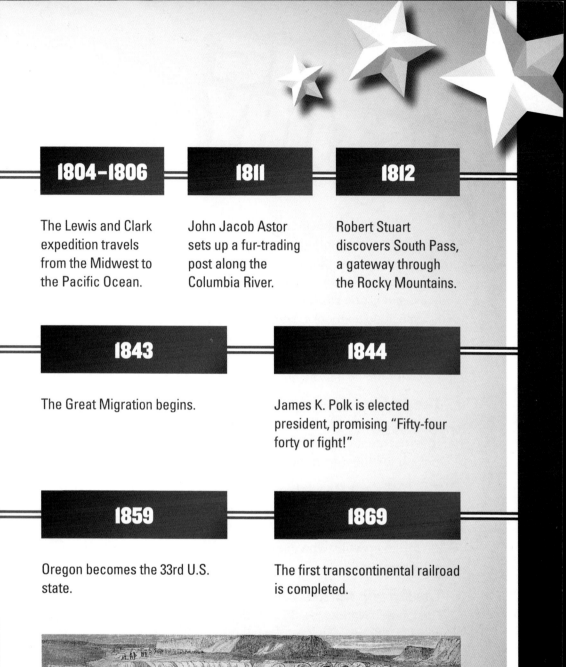

1804–1806

The Lewis and Clark expedition travels from the Midwest to the Pacific Ocean.

1811

John Jacob Astor sets up a fur-trading post along the Columbia River.

1812

Robert Stuart discovers South Pass, a gateway through the Rocky Mountains.

1843

The Great Migration begins.

1844

James K. Polk is elected president, promising "Fifty-four forty or fight!"

1859

Oregon becomes the 33rd U.S. state.

1869

The first transcontinental railroad is completed.

LIVING HISTORY

Primary sources provide firsthand evidence about a topic. Witnesses to a historical event create primary sources. They include autobiographies, newspaper reports of the time, oral histories, photographs, and memoirs. A secondary source analyzes primary sources, and is one step or more removed from the event. Secondary sources include textbooks, encyclopedias, and commentaries. To view the following primary and secondary sources, go to www.factsfornow.scholastic.com. Enter the keywords **Oregon Trail** and look for the Living History logo ∑:.

∑: The Ad That Tamed the Rockies

On February 13, 1822, businessman William H. Ashley placed an advertisement in the *Missouri Gazette & Public Advertiser*. He was looking for 100 men to help him trap animals for the fur trade.

∑: The Frémont Report

One of the most popular accounts of life on the Oregon Trail was the story of John Frémont's 1842–1843 journey. Frémont described the trip to his wife, who did the work of writing the report for publication.

∑: The Oregon National Historic Trail

The Oregon National Historic Trail preserves more than 2,000 miles (3,200 km) of the original paths traveled by pioneers as they headed westward.

∑: Thomas Jefferson's Instructions to Lewis and Clark

President Thomas Jefferson issued his instructions for the Lewis and Clark expedition in a handwritten note to the Corps of Discovery's leaders.

Books

Blumberg, Rhoda. *York's Adventures with Lewis and Clark: An African-American's Part in the Great Expedition*. New York: HarperCollins, 2003.

Friedman, Mel. *The California Gold Rush*. New York: Children's Press, 2010.

Galford, Ellen. *The Trail West: Exploring History Through Art*. Chanhassen, MN: Two-Can Publishing, 2005.

Manheimer, Ann S. *James Beckwourth: Legendary Mountain Man*. Minneapolis: Twenty-First Century Books, 2006.

Visit this Scholastic web site for more information on the Oregon Trail: www.factsfornow.scholastic.com Enter the keywords Oregon Trail

GLOSSARY

annexed (AN-ekst) took control of a country or territory

cholera (KAH-luh-ruh) a dangerous disease that causes severe vomiting and diarrhea, and is usually spread through contaminated water

colonies (KAH-luh-neez) areas settled by people from another country and controlled by that country

expedition (ek-spuh-DISH-uhn) a long trip made for a specific purpose, such as exploration

forded (FORD-id) crossed a river at a shallow point

frontier (fruhn-TEER) the far edge of a country, where few people live

geysers (GYE-zurz) underground hot springs that shoot boiling water and steam into the air

landmarks (LAND-mahrks) objects in a landscape that stand out

latitude (LAT-uh-tood) the distance north or south of the equator, measured in degrees

livestock (LIVE-stahk) animals kept or raised on a farm or ranch

Manifest Destiny (MAN-ih-fest DES-tuh-nee) a belief that America had a right to expand across the continent

migration (mye-GRAY-shuhn) movement from one region or country to another

missionaries (MISH-uh-ner-eez) people who travel to spread their religious faith among others

pioneers (pye-uh-NEERZ) people who explore unknown territory and settle there

telegraph (TEL-uh-graf) a device or system for sending messages over long distances using a code of electrical signals sent by wire or radio

transcontinental (trans-kon-tuh-NEN-tuhl) crossing a continent

INDEX

Page numbers in *italics* indicate illustrations.

ABOUT THE AUTHOR

Mel Friedman is an award-winning journalist and children's book author. He has academic degrees in history, political science, international affairs, and East Asian studies. As a journalist, he has written about advertising, media, constitutional law, economic competitiveness, the spread of nuclear weapons, and women's and children's health, among other issues. He speaks and reads Chinese and has taught English at a university in China. Friedman has written or cowritten more than two dozen children's books, both fiction and nonfiction. His children's nonfiction history books include titles on China, Thailand, Australia, U.S. history, Africa, and Antarctica. He and his wife and their daughter live in New York City and often rescue stray dogs.